BAROQUE AND ROCOCO

PAINTING OF THE WESTERN WORLD

BAROQUE AND ROCOCO

by Ian Barras Hill

Galley Press

Library of Congress Catalog Card No.
79-5368
ISBN 0-8317 0690 2
Manufactured in the Netherlands

Contents

Color illustrations

CHAPTER I

A time for change

Great art; a fusion of classical and romantic impulses tempered by perspective design and harmony – The atrophy of Renaissance styles and the advent of Mannerism (1520-1600) – The Counter Reformation and the spread of Catholicism in Europe – The influence of Venetian painters, Tintoretto and Titian and the new feeling for colour.

We learn from the history of the arts that the soul of man is in competition with itself. For each generation of artists one of two impulses is in ascendency: it rises up and colours man's creative vision. Will it be toward a formal, classical style (the design full of conventional realism), or will it be personal, passionate and expressive (full of the eccentricities of its creator)? The best art is often produced in times of equilibrium. The High Renaissance, the years 1495-1520, was such a time. The great painters, Leonardo da Vinci, Michelangelo and Raphael balanced their genius against the formal Renaissance techniques of perspective, design and harmony which they had learned as apprentices in the Florentine art workshops. Only Michelangelo in his later years lost his balance and allowed personal, expressive feelings to override the formal design.

Following the Renaissance decline the new generation developed a style called Mannerism which flourished in the years 1520-1600, and had international influence. The figures in Mannerist painting became agitated, and were rendered in disturbingly bright colours. The subject of painting became less important than the experimental way in which it was handled. It all seemed a chilling, logical conclusion to Michelangelo's last paintings in which realism was rejected in favour of distortion. Perspective, balance and harmony were deliberately flouted in favour of ostentation, drama and a kind of melancholic savagery. Though it did produce a few masterpieces, Mannerism was not a distinguished period of painting. Throughout the Mannerist era all of Europe was under the pressure of intense religious debates. The Catholic Church in Rome was reasserting its authority over the Protestant ideas of northern Europe. The Church looked in horror at the liberties taken by the Renaissance artists. It ordered the nude pictures in churches to have clothes painted on them, and it took a hard line on the position and duties of the artist in society, insisting that art should become religious propaganda once more.

In Rome, where this Counter Reformation pressure was the strongest, there was a sharp decline in the quality of art produced. It is claimed by some that the changes in Church patronage gave rise to Mannerism, and by others that they hastened the decline of Mannerism and gave birth to Baroque styles.

Statues on the colonnades of St Peter's Square, Rome by Gianlorenzo Bernini

Deposition, 1602-04
painting by Caravaggio
Rome, Pinacoteca Vaticana

Portrait of the lute-player,
Mascheroni
drawing by Annibale Carracci
Vienna, Graphische Sammlung
Albertina

Venetian art was little affected by Mannerism and by the Counter Reformation. The workshops of Veronese and Tintoretto continued to produce characteristically Venetian works with a feeling for colour and light. Venice was often visited by German, Flemish and Dutch painters who were so impressed by the Venetian feel for atmospheric lighting and colouring that they copied the style most successfully. A conscious revolt against Mannerism began in Florence and was growing stronger towards the final decade of the 16th century, but it was in Rome that the new style was to develop, a style that came to be known as Baroque.

Michelangelo Merisi, known as Caravaggio (c. 1571-1610) was born in Milan but travelled through northern Italy to settle in Rome. He was first employed by a cardinal at the Vatican who recognized his precocious talent. His harshly realistic work was a move away from the self-indulgent expressive style of the Mannerist school, it was a move toward classicism, toward the feeling that a deeper truth lies behind the appearance of things. Using a dramatic contrast between light and dark (characteristically, streams of bright sunlight cut diagonally through a dark room lighting up the faces and figures in action), Caravaggio drew upon the styles of the Renaissance, and began a whole new era of painting.

A family of painters from Bologna, the brothers Agostino and Annibale Carracci and their cousin, Lodovico (born 1557, 1560 and 1555) formed the other corner stone of the Baroque. The two brothers went on tours throughout northern Italy, and gained a Venetian feeling for colour and light from Veronese and Tintoretto and a sense of action struggling out of an atmosphere of gloom from Jacopo Bassano.

It is sometimes argued that Caravaggio and Annibale Carracci (the most important of the family) founded just another brief era of Classicism which quickly developed into the Baroque, and that Mannerism tempered by Classicism is the essence of the Baroque style. During the 17th and 18th centuries the national styles of painting showed great contradiction, some moving toward a classical approach and others toward personal expression. Most currents, however, had something of the Baroque, with each country and each painter adapting the Baroque inspiration to his own personal style.

Baroque emerged as a vigorous new style in painting, architecture and sculpture, as all three were often gathered together and integrated to strive towards "the grand effect" – majestic, imaginative and daring. Painting kept to the ground rules of accurate perspective, balanced design and realistic colour, but the astonishing use of light and internal illumination became the startling and expressive factor in each picture. Light was used to achieve illusions. The flicker or broadside of light suggested movement; the portrait, coming out of the gloom into light, added mood and character to the features of the subject. These changes happened over a period we can conveniently divide into Early Baroque (1585-1625), High Baroque (1625-1675) and Late Baroque (1675-1715).

8

CHAPTER II

Early Baroque 1595-1625

*Art as religious propaganda - The Vatican City as chief patron
- Rome, the nucleus of activity - Arrival of Caravaggio, the
eternal fugitive - The Carracci brothers and ceiling frescoes - The
Academy of Bologna - Valentin de Boulogne - Domenichino
and the development of landscape painting - Guercino.*

After the sack of Rome in 1527, when the artists of the
Renaissance had fled to the northern city-states of Italy, the
Catholic Church was restored stronger than ever before. As if
in an attempt to consolidate its Roman centre of St. Peter's and to
engender a greater confidence in the Church, a new respect for
Church paintings as objects of devotion was signalled by the
production of official guidebooks to Church art and museums.
This respect for painting was echoed in Florence where the
Academy of Fine Art was appointed to prevent the export or
destruction of its works of art. At the close of the 16th century the
Vatican's willingness to spend money on propagandist religious
painting once more attracted artists from all over Italy and Europe.
Undoubtedly the most important painters to arrive were
Caravaggio and Annibale Carracci.
Caravaggio had distinguished himself with collectors' paintings
such as *The Basket of Fruit* before beginning three large canvasses
on the life of St. Matthew for the Church. Whereas the Renaissance painters of a century before had found that tricks of perspective gave a greater sense of realism to a flat painting, so Caravaggio
discovered that the creative use of internal lighting could give a
painting an intense, almost tangible sense of reality. The figures
emerge from gloom by the fall of unnatural light; not natural light
and diffused sunlight, but a forced and abstract deluge of
illumination from no known source.
The paintings of Caravaggio were not readily accepted by the
Church on account of another innovation – his use of the
colloquial: the image of common man and familiar street scenes to
complement paintings of the saints. The features of holy men
were not idealized but were drawn from men in the streets. *The
Madonna with the Pilgrims* caused a sensation on account of the
dirty feet and torn clothing of figures kneeling in the foreground.
The Death of the Virgin was refused by the Carmelites because the
Virgin was shown with bare limbs, a swollen belly and pro-
nounced features.
There is something more starkly Classical than Baroque in
Caravaggio's paintings. Ironically, they deny the orthodox
religious view which they attempt to illustrate. The painter was
reputed to be a fiery and erratic character who quarrelled with the
authorities, was thrown into jail several times, killed a man in a

duel and was forced to flee through Naples, Malta, Sicily and back to Naples, painting considerable masterpieces in churches at these places, before dying himself aged 37. Caravaggio had no distinguished students, but he did have a considerable following, called Caravaggists, who continued his techniques, and dominated the styles of the Early Baroque.

Annibale began his career in Rome at the same time as Caravaggio. In order to remind his family of his humble beginnings in Bologna he painted *The Butcher's Shop*, an early depiction of low-life culture which shows tradesmen killing, weighing, cutting and hanging lurid sides of pork. He was credited with rediscovering the work of Correggio, a Renaissance painter of a century before whose painted ceilings and technique of internal illumination make him a great prophet of the Baroque style. It was a painted ceiling, that of the Farnese Palace, which brought enormous fame to Annibale Carracci and his brother, Agostino. On a barrelshaped ceiling, divided into panels with the panels separated by sculpture, they painted in fresco (paint applied to wet plaster) some love scenes from the classical poet, Ovid. The paintings are a beautiful blend of classicism and humanity. They made the same kind of impact on other artists as Masaccio's frescoes did nearly two centuries earlier. Annibale was called the best frescoist since Raphael, and for centuries after painters would come to see the work.

If Caravaggio introduced drama into painting then the Carracci brothers brought joy and enchantment. There is the same exuberance brought down to a human scale which we can see in the earlier works of the Venetians, Titian and Giorgione, when they attempted mythological subjects a century before.

Despite the pagan and erotic subject-matter, this group of frescoes found rapid favour with the authorities. They were so admired that they prompted decorative painting of walls and ceilings of palaces in Rome and all over Europe. But there was another reason for the spread of the Carracci style. Back in their hometown of Bologna, the Carracci had founded, in 1585, the Accademia degli Incamminati for students of art. They taught anatomy, drawing from living models, and a study of the great masters of the past. Among their celebrated pupils were Domenichino and Guido Reni. Bologna flourished as a centre of art, and close liaisons were formed with Rome.

The greatest of the Carracci, Annibale, died in Rome in 1609; he incurred a misleading reputation as a copier of the great masters, whilst his brilliant innovations were the result of detailed observations of nature and of live models. It was Annibale who evolved the heroic landscape style which preoccupied so many Baroque painters. His cousin Ludovico continued to run the Bologna Academy till his death in 1619.

Caravaggio and the Carracci gave rise to a second generation who developed the divergent and often contradictory possibilities of their master's work. A great many painters from northern Europe came to Rome and took off from Caravaggio. Bartolomeo Manfredi (c. 1580-1620/1) from Mantua began by forging

Study for a figure in the ceiling fresco of the Farnese Gallery, c. 1598 drawing by Annibale Carracci Paris, Musée National du Louvre

Judith beheading Holofernes, c. 1620
painting by Artemisia Gentileschi
Florence, Galleria degli Uffizi

St William of Aquitania receives the
monastic habit, 1620
painting by Guercino
Bologna, Pinacoteca Nazionale

Caravaggio pictures, but went on to originate a style called genre painting in which street characters in dimly lit rooms drank, gambled and brawled. It is said that this style found great favour with painters from Utrecht, France and Germany. A Frenchman, Moise Valentin (c. 1591-1632), called Valentin de Boulogne, was a clever exponent of this genre.

Orazio Gentileschi (c. 1562-1647) from Pisa knew Caravaggio, learned his style and carried it to Paris and London where he was the court painter to Charles I. His best painting, *Danae* (1621-2), shows an orange-hued nude reaching up to a shower of gold. She lays upon crushed white sheets, against a dark background. It surpasses anything Caravaggio could have done. But Orazio is said to have been surpassed himself by an energetic daughter, Artemisia (1593-1652). Her painting of *Judith beheading Holofernes* (c. 1620) is a particularly savage work in bright colours. She was involved in a famous rape case five or six years before, and it may have influenced her choice of subject matter.

Domenichino (1581-1641) trained under Lodovico Carracci in Bologna and worked under Annibale Carracci at the Farnese Palace. He picked up the Carracci interest in Raphael and classical masters, and his landscape painting had an enormous influence on Poussin and Claude Lorraine. Due to his neurotic and temperamental character he was unable to work easily with other artists. His paintings show a certain classical restraint and move toward the central Baroque style of many small figures scattered through a convoluted landscape. Domenichino's reputation has waned over the centuries, his work being overshadowed by that of Pietro da Cortona and Lanfranco.

Francesco Barbieri (1591-1661), known as Guercino or Squint-Eye, also trained under Lodovico Carracci at the Bolognese Academy, but he blended the style of Caravaggio with that of the Carracci. His early works contain crude and hastily painted figures in poor designs, and lit in patches. It was after his journey to Rome in 1621 that he took up the techniques of using light to create illusions. He turned to painting ceilings and the effects he achieved had an impact on Baroque decoration in general. Like many of these early imitators of Caravaggio and Carracci, he was swept aside by a new generation who carried the techniques very much further.

Toward the close of the Early Baroque period, 1625, there appears to be a certain dilution of the hard and contrasted style of Caravaggio. Orazio Riminaldi from Pisa with his *Martyrdom of St. Cecilia* (1615-20), moves away from Caravaggio to a desultory classicism. Carlo Saraceni (1579-1620), with his *Miracle of St. Zeno* (1618) regressed to a Renaissance form of classicism.

The faltering principles of classical Early Baroque were shared between the followers of Carracci in Bologna and the followers of Caravaggio in Rome. A third movement was emerging in Florence, so long silent since it had fielded the great names of Renaissance painting a century before. Florentine artists struggled against the old styles of Mannerism without coming across the new styles operating in Rome and Bologna.

CHAPTER III

The High Baroque in Italy and Holland, 1625-75

Bernini, architect, sculptor and central figure - Pietro da Cortona - Lanfranco - Guido Reni - Neapolitan painting - Jusepe de Ribera - Frans Hals and solid burghers - Rubens, painter, diplomat and giant of the Flemish Baroque - Dutch painters in England - Van Dyck, the gentleman courtier - Lely and the International style - Rembrandt's spirituality and humanity - The wooded scenes of Jacob van Ruisdael and Hobbema - Aelbert Cuyp - The Ostade brothers; frozen lakes and smoky taverns - Jan Steen, storybook fun and games - Ter Borch, domestic portraiture - Vermeer, a mystery wrapped in an enigma - De Hooch, shafts of sunlight through doors and courtyards.

Baldacchino, 1624-33
by Gianlorenzo Bernini
Rome, St Peter

Until the 19th century the word "Baroque" was a term of dismissive contempt for a style that was considered decorous, exaggerated and artificial. The German art historian Heinrich Wölfflin in his book *Renaissance und Barock* (1888) was among the first to attempt an identification and appreciation of the style. The Early Baroque saw the change from the contortions of Mannerism to more realistic human figures, often set in a tavern or against a landscape, usually part of a narrative; and the whole given dramatic effect by the illusionary use of lighting. The period of the High Baroque was the rise of painting as a complement to the new, audacious and decorative architecture.

Gianlorenzo Bernini (1598-1680), sculptor and architect of Rome, was the outstanding innovator of the High Baroque style. He was to his century what Michelangelo was to the century before. His early years were given to sculpture and a little painting, but he was encouraged to apply his creative imagination to architecture, to the internal design of churches, including the greatest of them all, St. Peter's at the Vatican; to fountains, staircases, tombs and monuments and to theatre design. He wholly embraced the decorative styles of the Baroque, invested them with great authority by his confident designs, and then took the styles to France, to the court of Louis XIV.

The Baroque period was churches, paintings and sculpture gathered into a more decorative ensemble. Not only the buildings, but the streets and squares, and even the man-made landscape gardens became part of the overall plan. Whereas Renaissance art provided us with a static and ideal viewpoint, the Baroque style invited our participation; encouraged us to walk around and through its architecture and sculpture, so that we may enjoy the many pleasing views.

St Bibiana, 1624-26
marble by Gianlorenzo Bernini
Rome, S. Bibiana

John the Baptist, c. 1640
painting by Guido Reni
London, Dulwich College,
Picture Gallery

The High Baroque opened with the exceptional equestrian statues of Francesco Mochi in the city of Piacenza, and moved forward upon Bernini's statuary which reproduced the fine texture of skin and hair, and even caught fleeting expressions on stone faces. Bernini designed the statue of Santa Bibiana in the church of that name in Rome. He also designed the modest facade, and Pietro da Cortona (1595-1669) painted frescoes inside that same church. This collaboration, albeit on an insignificant church, sparked the High Baroque into life.

Originally from Florence, Pietro invested vigorous theatricality and illusionism into fresco painting. His celebrated ceilings for the Barberini Palace are a marvel. We seem to look through the ceiling into an open sky: figures float in the air and appear to descend into the hall. Pietro's work became the forerunner to grand ceiling painting throughout Europe, including the French Palace of Versailles.

If Pietro da Cortona and Bernini brought the flamboyant and decorative side of the Baroque style to its climax, then Giovanni Lanfranco (1582-1647) achieved the classical balance. Lanfranco was from the northern city of Parma where he must have been familiar with the work of his townsman Correggio of a century earlier. It was said that the individual figures of Lanfranco's painted ceilings blend to form a harmonious whole, just as the voices of a choir blend in the music of Palestrina or Monteverdi. His mastery of ceiling illusions is so complete that centuries afterwards, and even allowing for the discolouring of paint, it is impossible to tell whether we are looking through the ceiling, or merely at a clever painting of the sky.

During the period of the High Baroque, Rome was attracting painters from all over Europe, and Kings were sending for Roman painters to decorate new palaces designed by Roman architects. Bologna, once the equal of Rome, began to fade in importance. A Bolognese painter with a considerable reputation (until savaged by the influential Victorian critic, John Ruskin) was Guido Reni (1575-1642). The Bolognese admirers of Reni continued to praise local painters and consider them superior to their Roman rivals. Reni produced rather wooden religious scenes, and with Domenichino, he began that sentimental tradition of painting the faces of saints with their eyes raised in holy ecstasy. Besides swooning saints, Reni developed a kind of romanticism such as *Atalanta and Hippomenes* (1615-25) which has a distinctive Mannerist feel about it. He is reputed to have been a virgin all his life with a neurotic fear of being poisoned, approached by an old woman or tricked with witchcraft. No doubt his unstable character accounts for the hint of dark mystery which make many of his paintings oddly popular.

By the period of the High Baroque, these various styles had been carried all over Europe and adapted to the individual artists or local tastes. Southern Italy was under Spanish domination, and so, through the Italian part of Naples, the Italian Baroque was taken up by visiting Spanish painters such as Jusepe de Ribera (1591-1652). Spanish painters generally have an eye for unpalatable

Rubens's son Nicolaas, 1625-27
drawing by Peter Paul Rubens
Vienna, Graphische Sammlung
Albertina

subjects, the grotesque, the freakish circus performer; it is a
tradition which has come down to Picasso in more recent times.
Ribera initiated a style of Italo-Spanish painting which is often
called Neapolitan.

The Baroque style was carried to northern Europe by the Dutch
painters Honthorst and Terbrugghen when they went back from
Rome to their Catholic town of Utrecht in Holland. Utrecht
became active in gloomy Caravaggist paintings of tavern and
brothel scenes. Frans Hals (1581/5-1666), who lived in Haarlem,
not far from Utrecht, adopted this style, but turned it to
commercial use. He obtained many commissions to paint groups
of soldiers who were all over Holland preparing to fight in the
wars against Spain. All the soldiers had to share equal positions of
importance, which gave these group portraits an artificial look.
But Hals' individual portraits are more deserving of our attention,
for he worked at capturing rather obvious expressions, particularly
moods such as laughter.

Dutch and Flemish (Belgian) painting became distinctive and
internationally important in the hands of a succession of masters.
Peter Paul Rubens (1577-1640) took the Venetian style off the wall
and put it on canvas, where he pursued a dynamic form of realism
with industrious determination. Rubens went straight to his
sources and travelled to Venice and Rome to learn from the
Renaissance and Early Baroque masters. On his return to Antwerp
in 1608 he embarked upon a celebrated career, not only as a
painter but as a diplomat and man of letters. He ran a huge
workshop where he and his apprentices dashed-off canvasses with
commercial bravado. He had an eye to public appetites, and painted rather too many suggestive rape scenes involving fleshy
women, or portraits with sentimental, over-large eyes. His landscapes have not the mood and perfection of his Flemish
contemporaries; they would seem to indicate excessive haste both
in the choice of subject and in its execution. Rubens' work is said
to be vulgar and insincere: it is widely admired, but rarely liked.
He is said to be the Painters' painter, for the influence his quick,
daring compositions had on later generations.

One of Rubens' many pupils was Sir Anthony van Dyck (1599-
1641), known as a court painter, but more recently admired for his
early work and his watercolours. He seems to have been a careful
and diplomatic painter who lived well by producing cleverly
idealized portraits of powerful people, which always retained some
of the character of the sitter. He spent much time travelling
between Holland, Paris and London, cultivating his patrons and
trying to advance his own reputation while under the shadow of
Rubens. Among Van Dyck's followers was Sir Peter Lely (1618-
80) who, like Van Dyck, came from Holland to London where he
lived sumptuously as a court painter. His work is often confused
with Van Dyck's, though Lely moved with the times. His austere
Commonwealth portraits gave way to more sensuous paintings of
Restoration ladies of the court.

The great name of Dutch painting was Rembrandt (1606-69). He
adapted the fashion of strong light and dark contrasts and applied

14

Self portrait, 1640, detail
painting by Rembrandt van Rijn
London, National Gallery

this technique to his many studies of domestic and social life. Our perception of Rembrandt's work is not always accurate owing to the varnishes used by him and by later generations, which have darkened many of his paintings out of recognition. His biographical details, his rise to wealth and reputation, the early death of his wife and children, and his bankruptcy, are the stuff of legend, but in truth he seems a remote and inaccessible personality. By contrast with Rubens' flamboyance and love of melodrama Rembrandt seems a very cerebral painter with a high technical skill somewhat wasted upon his posed and rather bloodless subjects. He painted over sixty self-portraits through which we can see his rise to success, and his fall to a time of mellow introspection.

Rembrandt's painting *The Nightwatch*, though a masterpiece of design and technique, is more an historic illustration, than a work of art. It is not in any way an illumination of life, an insight into human values or a comment upon the folly of the times. It is an impartial record, almost a photograph of a daily event. This uncontroversial style accompanied a general change in fashion on Dutch painting. The dramatic aspects of Baroque were abandoned for a quieter, classical approach and for less demanding subjects: still-life, landscapes and historical subjects. Rembrandt was perhaps the greatest etcher of his time. He picked up from Dürer and Lucas van Leyden, and learned to mix varying techniques in one composition. His etchings have a free and imaginative style which proved a great influence on later generations.

Though Rembrandt's studied realism was a move away from earlier, flamboyant styles, his reputation became victim of an increasing classicism in painting fashion. After his death, his work was dismissed as vulgar, naturalist painting and for a century the classicist rejection of his manner influenced his biographers, so that they wrote of him as a vain and greedy man. The English painter Joshua Reynolds is credited with starting a revival of English interest in Rembrandt, and by the 19th century his work was attracting the attention it deserves.

Mid-century Dutch and Flemish painting, in the hands of scores of competent draughtsmen, slowly abandoned the familiar themes and narratives and moved toward a style of photographic realism. Here were stormy skies, trees crowding over a ruin, ships upon an estuary, windmills, feasts in houses, peasant cottages, portraits of dignitaries and all manner of subjects upon the general principle that life is not a harmony of simple, elusive forces, as the Renaissance painters believed, but rather a matter of irreconcilable diversities. All colour was drained out of paintings, which became imbued with a monochromatic contrast in addition to the internal contrasts of the subject matter, where deliberately low horizons provided the opportunity for a great deal of angry cloud.

Jacob van Ruisdael (1628-82) is often considered the greatest Dutch landscape painter. He was influenced by the Haarlem landscapist Cornelisz Vroom but became preoccupied with trees which he clad with personality and promoted to the centre piece of his paintings. He moved from thick, dark colours to brighter

Return of the prodigal son, 1636
etching by Rembrandt van Rijn
Cambridge, Fitzwilliam Museum

Avenue at Middelharnis, c. 1689
painting by Meindert Hobbema
London, National Gallery

complexions and took to more distant views of Haarlem and
panoramas of the Dutch countryside over which clouds rage. His
close friend Meindert Hobbema (1638-1709) often painted the
same views but preferred watermills and less demanding
landscapes without the cloud. His painting *Avenue at Middelharnis*
is an arresting and unforgettable painting.

Aelbert Cuyp (1620-91) painted more poetic landscapes,
remarkable for their luminous quality. His pictures of resting cattle
silhouetted against the sky bring a rare note of tranquillity to an
agitated age. His father, Jacob Cuyp, was a notable portraitist. The
brothers Adriaen van Ostade (1610-85) and Isack van Ostade (1621-
49) were known for their "genre" painting: scenes of Dutch
peasant life. Adriaen painted over a thousand small works, mostly
on wood, as well as sketches and watercolours. It is thought that
along with A. Brouwer, he was a student of Frans Hals. His
paintings of peasants tend toward caricature and yet they are very
engaging. Isack was known for his winter scenes and for cottage
or tavern scenes with horses. His pictures of skaters and sleigh
riders attract deserving attention. Many of his works show a
mastery of smoky or misty atmospheres.

Willem Kalf (1619-93) absorbed the chiaroscuro of Rembrandt
and the satisfying colouring of Vermeer, which he applied to his
still-life compositions. His work was in great demand, and it
brings home to us the sumptuous banquets and possessions
enjoyed by the 17th-century Dutch middle-classes.

With a reputation a little inferior to that of Frans Hals and
Rembrandt, the Dutch painter Jan Steen (1626-79) introduced the
neglected element of humour into Dutch painting. Steen married
the daughter of the painter Jan van Goyen and lived at the Hague
for some years, then in turn at Delft, Haarlem and Leiden. His
landscapes with winter and tavern scenes seem to owe something
to the Ostade brothers, but he diversified and captured many
aspects of Dutch daily life, as in *The Doctor's Visit* or *The Village*

16

School. His figures, particularly his children, have delightful expressions, and his paintings have a characteristic technical excellence.

Gerard Ter Borch (1617-81) was a precocious painter who travelled through England, Italy and Spain where he must have become acquainted with the more vigorous Baroque styles, but his paintings show a Dutch moderation. He produced many portraits and group scenes, and his works seem a subtle treatment of colour and light, until compared to the work of Vermeer.

A brilliant diversion from the mainstream is represented by the work of two painters from Delft, Pieter de Hooch and the incomparable Jan or Johannes Vermeer (1632-75). Not till the last hundred years was Vermeer known at all; his paintings were formally attributed to others. Only 30 or 35 pictures are known to be by this shadowy figure, so unforthcoming that his probable self-portrait in *Allegory of Painting* is a back view. But his work (and not De Hooch's) is giving rise to great excitement this century. Because of its analytical detail it is often compared to scientific investigations of the time, and on account of its mysterious mood it is seen as an evocation of 17th century mysticism. Vermeer painted indoor scenes often of middle-class life, usually choosing a domestic setting which is not generalized, but is kept very personal. We feel that we are glimpsing into the family life of the artist not as a stranger, but through his own eyes. The people and furniture are deployed with telling significance, as if in tune with hidden principles of decorum in the refined and enclosed universe of Vermeer's society. The chief figure of each painting is given a single prop with which to indicate their relationship with their environment; it might be a musical instrument, a jug, a wine-glass or commonly a letter. The paintings themselves are rendered with a studied attention to textures and to the incidence of direct and reflected light. He painted two known landscapes, probably from a window. His celebrated townscape, *View of Delft*, with its horizontal bands of sand, water, city and sky, is said to have set the style for future landscape painting.

Pieter de Hooch (1629-84) painted streets and courtyards with a developed sense of domestic order and atmospheric mood, and has not impressed the contemporary imagination as much as his fellow painter Vermeer. This great era of Dutch and Flemish painting was extinguished by the French invasion of 1672. Many painters moved to England and Germany, or, with the subsequent collapse of the Dutch economy, stopped painting altogether.

The styles of the mid-century have been variously called heroic-classical or Baroque. Faced with such individuality and diversity it is difficult to demonstrate any stylistic affinities with Italian art of this same period. Northern European painting was based on the weaving of two or three incompatible threads: the bright, sensuous mythologies of Rubens, the near black and white paintings of city low-life, fishing boats on estuaries, poverty or laughter in taverns and cottages, formal portraits, single portraits of humourless dignitaries, and the domestic scenes of effortless elegance by Vermeer.

Allegory of Painting, c. 1665
painting by Jan Vermeer
Vienna, Kunsthistorisches Museum

CHAPTER IV

The High Baroque in France and Spain

Simon Vouet's theatrical scene-painting - Landscapes of Poussin; pathos tempered by Classicism - Le Brun's factory of decorative schemes - Claude Lorraine; antique palaces and the Roman Campagna - The Le Nain brothers - Georges de la Tour; penitent calm by candle light - The intense El Greco; elongated distortions of a mystical visionary - The sentimentalized beggar boys of Murillo - Zurbaran - Juan Valdes Leal - Francisco Pacheco - The objective realism of Velasquez at the Court of Philip IV.

The Baroque style is said to have arrived in Paris with the return of Simon Vouet (1590-1649) from Rome. He brought with him an Italian Early Baroque style drawn from Lanfranco and Guido Reni, and made himself a reputation painting huge altarpieces and decorating the insides of palaces. His undeserved hold on French painting was shaken, but not lost, upon the return of a brilliant compatriot.

Nicolas Poussin (1594-1665) was born in northern France but spent most of his life in Rome which he knew to be the centre of European painting. He was unimpressed by the Caravaggist style of slanting illumination; his own painting had a more natural distribution of light which goes back to the Renaissance painters. His interest was in classical sculpture and in the painting of the great masters, particularly Raphael and the Venetian school of Titian and Bellini. Whereas the Parisian painters like Vouet used light undercoats which give a bright artificiality to painting, Poussin used reddish undercoats, which are now beginning to show through and darken his early pictures.

After fifteen years in Rome during which he developed a contempt for French culture, his own reputation was so high that Cardinal Richelieu invited him back to join the French Royal Academy. It was a disaster. His own reputed arrogance could not submit to the trivial commissions for palace tapestries and book-covers. He was accustomed to choosing his own subjects, so he left abruptly to go back to Rome. It was during this second and final stay there that he developed a pagan philosophy, and, in the French tradition, used his reputation as a painter to promulgate his less acceptable personal views.

Poussin's work has a monumental gravity; all the drama and authority of religious themes transferred to classical subjects. His very innocent figures disport against landscapes of aquaducts, inland cliffs and golden clouds. His style is placed clearly between the Baroque and the French Classicism of a century later. In France

Holy Family with St Elizabeth and St John, c. 1640
drawing by Nicolas Poussin
Windsor Castle

The expressions, 1698, detail
from "Traité des passions"
by Charles Le Brun

Blacksmith at his forge
painting by Louis Le Nain
Paris, Musée National du Louvre

he is regarded as the greatest painter of the 17th century, and perhaps France's greatest. In the 19th century Cézanne announced his intention to take up Poussin's style.

The period of the High Baroque was the slow transfer of the artistic initiative from Rome towards Paris. Charles Le Brun (1619-90) was largely responsible for this move. He studied with Simon Vouet and went to Rome with Poussin, but developed a taste for themes of imperialist grandeur which found him employment with Louis XIV. Le Brun was awarded commissions to decorate palaces, among them the Palace of Versailles.

For thirty years Le Brun supervised most of the art commissioned by the French government. His influence drew all the styles together to give French art its characteristic unity, which is said to be academic and propagandist. The flamboyant and illusionist tendencies of Baroque art were adapted to a classical grandeur known as the Louis XIV style.

An even greater French classicist was Claude Lorraine (1600-82) who affected a synthesis of Flemish landscape with Italian lighting. He put the sun upon canvas so that we are dazzled by it. His harbours of ships and palaces along the shore are saturated with soft, golden light. This obvious positioning of the sun contributes a powerful sense of dawn or dusk, of passing time, which in turn gives the poetic scene a feeling of melancholy and of great antiquity. Claude Lorraine had the greatest influence on Turner and the English Romantic movement of the early 19th century.

Not all French painting followed the Poussin style of heroic mythology; there remained an active rural school of realists who passed the tradition on to Millet in the 19th century. The brothers Antoine, Louis and Mathieu Le Nain opened a workshop in Paris where they painted peasant subjects. They seem to have collaborated on many paintings and it is not worth the trouble to distinguish their individual contributions. In later life Mathieu took to portraits and huge compositions. The acknowledged genius of the family, Louis Le Nain (1593-1648), painted *A Blacksmith at his Forge* which hung in the Louvre to influence 19th century artists.

An almost forgotten painter, Georges de La Tour (1593-1652), from eastern France, has been given a disproportionate coverage in artbooks over recent years. He developed a style distinctly his own in which familiar saints with glassy features like those of a doll are caught in an enriching glow of candlelight. His secular figures, beggars and peasants are often rendered as "characters" with wispy hair and rugged faces. His better figures, with their slow gestures, and half-caught in shadow, have a pleasing dignity about them which put us in mind of Vermeer.

The influence of the Italian Baroque on Spain and Portugal was very different. The Iberian Peninsula was little affected by the Italian Renaissance of the 16th century; the Gothic and Moorish styles prevailed through to the times of Mannerism and the Baroque. The painter El Greco (1541-1614), born in Crete which then belonged to Venice, began to paint in the old Byzantine styles but was impressed by the Mannerists, by Titian and by

The Annunciation, 1596-1600
painting by El Greco
Villanueva y Geltrú, Museo Balaguer

Jesus in the Temple, 1686
painting by Juan Valdes Leal
Madrid, Museo del Prado

Michelangelo. He went to Spain and was commissioned to paint great altarpieces, which he did with acid colours and a stylish eccentricity which has made his work distinctive. He ignored the chiaroscuro of Caravaggio, and had little interest in the Baroque concern for realism, but the dynamism and apparent action of his figures are part of the Baroque inspiration. El Greco had few imitators and was overshadowed by the genius of Velasquez. Murillo (1617-82) began his career painting at fairgrounds but moved to a more acceptable style after seeing the work of Titian, Rubens and Velasquez. There remained in his work the flaw of excessive sentimentality, making sweet scenes out of harsh circumstances. His charming beggar-children found great favour with the Spanish public but continue to offend the art historian. The rise of Murillo's popular style eclipsed the mystical realism of Francisco de Zurbaran (1598-1664), who was said to have derived his style from sculpture. Whereas Murillo may put us in mind of Raphael with paintings like *Eliezer and Rebecca* or the larger *Immaculate Conception*, Zurbaran, with his *Adoration of the Shepherds* hints at Michelangelo.

The most Baroque of painters was Juan Valdes Leal (1622-90). He painted in the chiaroscuro style but used quick, impressionist brushstrokes, and a manner called "temperamental painting", The mainstream of Spanish painting was in the hands of Herrera the Elder (c. 1590-1655) and Francisco Pacheco (1564-1654). Herrera and his son dabbed with an impressionistic spontaneity, but Pacheco criticized this method of detached strokes. Pacheco's pupil, Velasquez, who became his son-in-law, began painting, under instruction, in the heavily contrasting chiaroscuro of the time, but fortunately for the world, he ignored his master's objections and took to the technique of quick, impressionistic strokes.

Diego Velasquez (1599-1660) may well have studied under Herrera the Elder before he went to Pacheco, and certainly has achieved a heroic synthesis between the contrasting styles of these two painters. Pacheco was only an indifferent painter of the Mannerist school but he produced important biographical material on his illustrious son-in-law as well as books on the theory of painting. His value as a teacher consisted in his setting the reluctant young Diego to draw and paint from life models for five years.

Velasquez' early paintings of religious or domestic scenes in the chiaroscuro and illusionistic style usually feature a prominent still-life, a collection of food or utensils thrown together in interesting ways. He often used kitchen scenes, of which *Old Woman Frying Eggs* is a famous example. The painting has a posed and static quality and a flatness of perspective, but it is an arresting composition of subtle and fascinating detail.

He was appointed a court painter and met Rubens, whose taste for rich decoration he adopted. About this time he modified his chiaroscuro and produced lighter backgrounds for his figures. A visit to Italy seemed to have impressed him for he is known to have admired Titian's work and copied Tintoretto's paintings in Venice, and then sketched Michelangelo's figures off the walls of

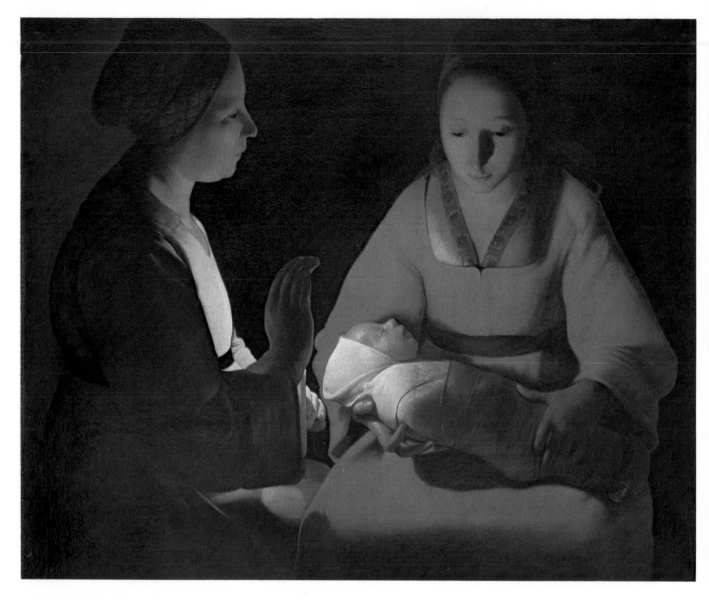

1. Nicolas Poussin
The poet's inspiration, c. 1630
Canvas, 94 x 70 cm
Hanover, Niedersächsische
Landesgalerie

It was in Rome and initially under
Domenichino that the Frenchman,
Poussin, developed a taste for landscaped mythologies. He was
invited back to Paris where Vouet's
work was the fashion and he left in
disgust. Most of his work shows
the influence of Raphael. It has
Venetian colouring and borrows
from Veronese. Poussin has come
down to us as one of the greatest
French masters of the High
Baroque style.

2. Georges de La Tour
The Newborn Child, 1646-48
Canvas, 76 x 91 cm
Rennes, Musée des Beaux-Arts

The chiaroscuro (light and shadow)
techniques of Caravaggio were taken
to Holland by two travelling Dutch
artists. Georges de La Tour was a
Frenchman who exploited the possibilities by producing many shadowy
scenes, frequently lit by a single
candle. In his search for simplicity the
figures lost all personality and became
like dolls. Despite these short-
comings, his reputation is in the
ascendency and his work is
frequently reproduced.

4. Mathieu Le Nain (attributed)
The gardener, 1655-60
Canvas, 93 x 120 cm
Cologne, Wallraf-richartz-Museum

The enigmatic brothers, Mathieu,
Antoine and Louis Le Nain frequently
worked on each other's canvases and
so it is scarcely possible to differen-
tiate their individual work. They
usually worked in the Dutch tradition, producing scenes of peasant life.
This painting is almost a still-life of
figures. It has a gloomy and ritualistic
mood – all eyes upon the gardener's
presentation of a flower. Perhaps it is
a declaration of love.

3. Antoine Le Nain (attributed)
Family reunion, 1642
Copper, 40 x 32 cm
Paris, Musée National du Louvre

The gentlemen of Antoine's family group – red nosed and watery eyed – are enjoying the occasion, but the bored young woman with the song book, her fingers in delicate display, is not in the spirit.
There is something of Hals in the portraits, and something Dutch about this celebration of inebriation.

5. Moise Valentin (Valentin de Boulogne)
Concert at the bas-relief, 1620-22
Canvas, 173 x 214 cm
Paris, Musée National du Louvre

Valentin was a French painter who established himself in Rome and became a friend of Poussin. His style is after Caravaggio and Manfredi. A significant number of Baroque paintings are of tavern and brothel scenes. Scenes of public and domestic life are known as genre paintings. They spread to Holland through the Catholic town of Utrecht, but the subjects had little appeal to English painters.

7. Simon Vouet
Psyche and Amor, 1626
Canvas, 112 x 165 cm
Lyon, Musée des Beaux-Arts

The Early Baroque style is said to have entered France upon Vouet's return from Rome to Paris. He was hugely popular in his day for portraits and altarpieces, though his skills may seem ordinary when compared with the best of Italian painters at his time. It all suggests that this fame rests upon his position as an importer of a new trend in painting. This classically restrained canvas seems of a different age and not consistent with the humanizing figures of the Baroque.

6. Hyacinth Rigaud
The artist's mother in two poses, 1695
Canvas, 81 x 101 cm
Paris, Musée National du Louvre

With its bull-neck and sad eyes it is not a flattering portrait and most certainly must be a likeness. Rigaud was the official court painter to two French Kings, Louis the XIV and XV. His formal portraits are careful attempts at flattery but retain sufficient elements of the original character. We may appreciate that artists in this time and beyond had little choice in their subject matter and in the use of free, interpretive expression. Rigaud is among the official portrait painters whose duties were like that of an official photographer.

8. Antoine Watteau
The Embarkation for Cythera, 1718
(second version)
Canvas, 128 x 193 cm
Berlin, Schloss Charlottenburg

It took the genius of Watteau to
break the constraints of academicism
which was subjugating French art. He
was influenced by theatre so that his
figures disport against a backdrop
which forms a magical balance
between painted scenery and awesome
landscape. The scene is inspired by
outdoor pageants conducted by the
French courtiers who would take
instruments out into parks in order to
enact romantic fantasies. Watteau
created beautiful images of a delicate
and ephemeral world, infusing them
with delicious nostalgia.

9. Antoine Watteau
Gilles, 1719-21
Canvas, 184 x 149 cm
Paris, Musée National du Louvre

The Italian theatre tradition of the
Commedia del'Arte with its stereoty-
pical characters enabled painters to
attempt interpretations. Gilles was
believed to be a sensitive and melancholy clown. Watteau makes him a
guarded, hesitant personality, perhaps
waiting for applause at the end of an
act. His posture summarizes the uni-
versal characters of all clowns, actors
and performers, that of helpless
deference. He neglects to participate
in the humour of his friends, but
stands respectfully for our attention.
There is a sad contrast between the
faintly ridiculous costume and the
sombre expression.

10. Nicolas de Largillière
The family of Louis XIV, 1709
Canvas, 129 x 162 cm
London, Wallace Collection

A portrait painter who did not aspire
to the heights of Rigaud, Largillière
was trained in Antwerp and brought
Flemish character to his work. He
served under Peter Lely in England
before going to Paris where he painted the families of the wealthy middle-
classes. This group portrait of the
King's family has a structured dispo-
sition of figures which looks back to
Renaissance techniques. The eye is
carried from figure to figure by way of
stray gestures or glances. It is a considered painting and rewarded by a
little time and attention despite the
look of fixed distrust by the King.

11. Charles Le Brun
Chancellor Séguier, 1660
Canvas, 295 x 357 cm
Paris, Musée National du Louvre

A pupil of Poussin and Vouet, Le Brun rose to a position of dictatorial power under the French King Louis XIV. To support the King's political programme, French art became uniform and propagandist. We may sense the prevailing mood of hierarchy and authority in this painting, where the subservient figures are decorative and dehumanized. Even the sensitive horse seems nervous of the illustrious rider whose black looks of smug disdain are echoed by the dark clouds behind him.

12. Jean Baptiste Chardin

Auguste-Gabriel Godefroy, c. 1738
Canvas, 68 x 76 cm
Paris, Musée National du Louvre

Chardin invested his still-life paintings with a sense of harmonious formality and achieved marvellous effects with colour. His paintings of bread and wine are rich evocations of substance and flavour. The young man of this portrait has been caught at an intimate moment. His hands rest naturally on the desk and he watches his spinning top with a look of child-like absorption. There are depths to this painting that are conspicuously absent in similar portraits by the Englishman, Joshua Reynolds. It is instructive to compare Chardin's sense of integrity with portraits by Maurice de La Tour.

13. Jean Marc Nattier the Younger

Madame Bouret as Diana, 1745
Canvas, 138 x 105 cm
Lugano, Collection Bornemisza-Thyssen

The French court of Louis XV flirted with mythological parallels. It was Nattier's position to flatter the ladies by portraying them as favoured goddesses. A bow, a quiver and a leopard-skin has tranformed the redoubtable Madame Bouret to something a little less transitory, the Greek Diana. We are acquainted with illusions that mislead powerful people, when pampered court beauties identify themselves with mythical huntresses. Was this the French conceit which gave rise to Napoleon?

14. Jean Baptiste Chardin
Lady sealing a letter, 1733
Canvas, 144 x 144 cm
Berlin, Schloss Charlottenburg

A French painter of still-life and domestic scenes, Chardin was in the tradition of the Dutch masters, and Vermeer in particular, while his countrymen were swept-up with the fashion of French Rococo. He achieved a restrained kind of naturalism, always reluctant to display his own feelings in a painting. The relaxed concentration of the couple here, as they lean towards eachother to draw wax off the candle, gives an intimate proximity to the scene. It is typical of Chardin's work that we sense an intelligent and generous mind behind the painting.

15. François Boucher
Miss Louise O'Murphy. (L'Odalisque).
1745-48
Canvas, 52 x 64 cm
Paris, Musée National du Louvre

When the English painter, Sir Joshua Reynolds visited Boucher in his studio, he was shocked to discover that Boucher painted from imagination and without models. The painter explained that he found it necessary to work from models when a student but he had not needed models since that time. But this girl was an exception. She was Louise O'Murphy, a pretty Irish lass who became the mistress of Louis XV when she was only sixteen. A great favourite of the court, chiefly through pin-up poses such a this, her lissom form made popular and acceptable the depiction of backs and bottoms in Rococo boudoir painting. To an age still recovering from the Baroque assault of Rubens' fleshy nudes, such

paintings had to be humerous, playful confections touched off by a powder-soft erotism. Diderot, the essayist, extolled the virtues of Miss O'Murphy in a Salon review of 1767: "A completely naked woman stretched out on pillows, legs astride, offering the most voluptuous head, the most beautiful back, the finest buttocks…?

16. Maurice Quentin de La Tour
Self-portrait, c. 1760
Pastel, 64 x 53 cm
Amiens, Musée de Picardie

Painting with pastels achieved great respectability in France. Maurice was something of a society painter who was moved to capture sweet caricatures. His portraits are lively but somewhat disingenuous. Like the pavement portraitists of the tourist towns, he contrived the features to an appropriate mood. He tends to flatter his sitters with an excess of charm. His self-portrait reveals humour and affability in suspiciously large quantities!

17. Jean Honoré Fragonard
Invocation à l'Amour, 1780-88
Canvas
Orleans, Musée des Beaux-Arts

Fragonard is remembered as the
painter of romantic confections. Much
of his work was set around amorous
intrigues and decorations. Like
Boucher he was obligated to a mistress of the king, and his work shows
a striving to please. His figures are
more dynamic than Boucher's; they
reach and leap and swing. The subject
matter is in keeping with Fragonard's
technique which was one of rapid
improvisation.

18. Jean Honoré Fragonard
Small cascade at Tivoli, c. 1760
Canvas, 73 x 60 cm
Paris, Musée National du Louvre

Fragonard spent five years in Rome
viewing the ruins. Powerful classical
inspiration was never far from his
mind and he toyed with the melancholic moods afforded by sights of
antique grandeur, before his successes
in Paris. The puny figures contending
with the vast indifference of nature
are the stuff of the later, romantic
movement in painting. The black
abyss, the ageless rock walls, the roar
of spilt water, all speak of a deep
romantic sensibility which was sup-
pressed for a lifetime in the royal
court.

19. Louis-Michel van Loo
Denis Diderot, 1767
Canvas
Paris, Musée National du Louvre

One of the famous Van Loo family
which spanned the century, Louis
Michel, son of Jean Baptiste van Loo,
took French art to Spain, whereas his
brother Charles-Amedée represented
the family in Prussia, settling finally in
Berlin. His portrait of this influential
man of French literature has imitations of Romantic sentiments,
where a sensitive man of letters is por-
trayed with an appropriate expression.
When the portrait painter aims for
the anticipated expression it robs the
portrait of depth.

21. Hubert Robert
Garden of Versailles, 1775
Canvas, 124 x 191 cm
Versailles, Musée National

Robert was a friend of the Roman
painters of ruins, Pannini and
Piranesi, but most of all he caught the
style of his friend Fragonard. He had
an interest in formal parks and gardens; he was a landscape gardener
himself. This painting is permeated
with neoclassical concerns of order
and disorder, of formal design and
organic freedom.
A garden must be a balance of bridled
foliage set in geometric arrangements.
The landscaping of a park was a creative and artistic entertainment, and as
this painting shows, was a time for
considerable public participation.

20. Orazio Gentileschi
The luteplayer, c. 1626
Canvas, 108 x 87.8 cm
Washington D.C., National Gallery of Art

Gentileschi was a friend of Caravaggio and developed a style that was a decided improvement upon that of his friend. He travelled to Paris and to London, and he is credited with bringing the beautiful new styles of the Early Baroque to the English capital. He is said to have brought a Tuscan poeticism to the Caravaggio style of cold realism. He lightened the colours and softened the gestures of the figures. For all his skills this painting has an awkward and unbalanced feel about it. The excess of drapery carries unnecessary overtones of religious passion.

22. Caravaggio
The Vocation of St. Matthew, c. 1600
Canvas, 328 x 348 cm
Rome, S. Luigi dei Francesi, Cappella
Contrarelli

This is one of three paintings commissioned to illustrate the life of St.
Matthew. The technique of contrasts
between light and dark called chiaroscuro, which brings depth and solidity
to the scene, was a considerable
influence on a century of painting.
The painter's use of ordinary and
sympathetic figures to represent saints
was considered a scandal at the time
and led to the rejection of several
paintings for churches.

23. Annibale Carracci
Triumph of Bacchus and Ariadne,
1595-1605
Fresco
Rome, Palazzo Farnese

Assisted by his brothers, Annibale
Carracci decorated the barrel-vaulted
ceiling of the palace, illustrating
mythological subjects from the love
poems of Ovid.
Here we find a sympathy and an exuberance with the living world. This
decorated ceiling helped to launch the
style called Baroque. It led to a
fashion for painted ceilings all over
Europe.

24. Giovanni Battista Piazzetta
Rebecca at the well, c. 1740
Canvas, 102 x 137 cm
Milan, Pinacoteca di Brera

Piazzetta moved from Bologna to
Venice where he introduced a sponta-
neous lighter and more decorative feel
to the Baroque style. Clearly he was
under the influence of Rembrandt and
Dutch painting in general. He was a
wood-carver and ceiling painter, and
he left a large number of drawings.

25. Cristofano Allori
Judith with the head of Holofernes, 1613
Canvas, 139 x 116 cm
Florence, Palazzo Pitti, Galleria
Palatina

Allori was from Florence, a city which
had little to contribute to the Baroque
era. It is an irony that it should have
been a Florentine who painted this
masterpiece in the Baroque style
which may well be the best Italian
painting of the century. We can only
guess at the fine paintings he would
have given the world if he had not
died in his early forties.

26. Pietro da Cortona
Allegory of Peace, 1633-39
Fresco ceiling, detail
Rome, Palazzo Barberini

Along with Bernini, Pietro was one of
the founders of the High Baroque. He
gave six years to painting the ceiling
of the Barberini Palace in a light vigorous style which has earned him the
name of the Italian Rubens. Though
the style of the Baroque is difficult to
define, the ceiling paintings in which
foreshortened figures float up into an
imaginary sky, seem to be the very
essence of the Baroque sensibility.

27. Canaletto
The Doge returning to Venice, 1729
Canvas, 182 x 259 cm
Milan, Collection of Aldo Crespi

A significant departure from the
Baroque scenes with figures are the
many townscapes. It is a typically
Venetian subject, and perhaps the best
known of Canaletto's works. He
developed a method of projecting the
image of a scene upon paper which he
sketched. It formed the basis of a
canvas back at his studio. Canaletto's
achievements are diluted by the fre-
quency of similar techniques. It is
probable that he thought of himself as
a recorder of scenes rather than an
interpreter.

28. Giovanni Battista Tiepolo
America (Continental allegory), 1750-53
Fresco, detail
Würburg, Residenz Hall

Tiepolo is often considered the last of
a long line of Italian masters. He was
commissioned to paint ceilings of
palaces for which he adopted free,
expressive figures which he painted in
light tones and pale colours. He had a
marvellous confidence in recreating
histories and mythologies in compel-
ling designs. All women were queens,
and all men were bristling heroes. He
was in the habit of painting small
samples, which if approved were painted on ceilings by assistants.

29. Pietro Longhi
The rhinoceros, 1751
Canvas, 62 x 50 cm
Venice, Ca'Rezzonico

Longhi was a popular and much
reproduced painter in his day but his
work seems to us a little obvious and
lacks the imagination of Tiepolo. The
group of masked figures do not sit
well together and seem like a collection of children's dolls. And yet we
cannot escape the looming and ambi-
guous symbolism of the rhinoceros
itself, well to the foreground and
seeming like part of another picture.
It is a hornless baby, chewing straw
with unconcern. The artist has drawn
our attention to it but offers no
explanations.

30. Jusepe de Ribera
Boy with a club-foot, 1652
Canvas, 164 x 92 cm
Paris, Musée National du Louvre

The lower half of the Italian peninsula
was under the domination of Spain,
and Spanish painters who settled in
Naples took to the Baroque styles.
Jusepe married the rather brutal
Spanish realism to the graceful inven-
tiveness of the Carracci to produce his
own style. One would not expect a
crippled boy to be so cheerful. This
little paradox gives some psychologi-
cal depth to the painting, which has
made it very popular.

31. Diego Velasquez
The Infanta Doña Margarita of Austria,
c. 1660
Canvas, 212 x 147 cm
Madrid, Museo del Prado

So often in Spain a painter comes forward whose style is a significant departure from that of his contemporaries. Velasquez synthesized many influences and produced a style of fluid realism. His work as a court painter obliged him to do formal portraits of uninteresting people. He was early in his use of impressionistic brushstrokes with which he rendered the highlights on fabrics. The princess of this portrait looks so vulnerable in her ridiculous gowns of state, and a little nervous of the painter.

32. Diego Velasquez
The Rokeby Venus, 1649-50
Canvas, 123 x 177 cm
London, National Gallery

Art historians have searched for the visual inspiration of the masterpiece which was probably painted during a trip to Italy, but it seems certain that Velasquez painted from a model. The flesh colouring and draped fabrics are particularly convincing, though it is obvious that she would not be seeing herself in the glass, she would be looking at us! This century has seen a developing interest in the works of Velasquez; his paintings are fetching the highest prices at auctions, and he is sometimes spoken of as the greatest of all painters.

33. Goya
Blindman's buff, c. 1787
Canvas (tapestry design), 269 x 350 cm
Madrid, Museo del Prado

Goya began his career in the shadow of the great Italian, Tiepolo, who had lived his last years in Spain. His early years as a designer of tapestries and as a court painter were not distinguished, but he was deeply affected by the experiences of the savage wars which swept Spain, and he turned later to a declamatory, propagandist style. This early tapestry design with its bright colours and studied elegance was done at a time in Goya's life when he was moving towards a Neo- Classical style. His famous portrait of the Duchess of Alba from around this time is typical of the stiff and formal sense of elegance in the Spanish court.

34. William Hogarth
Mariage à la Mode Nº 2 (Shortly after
the marriage), 1743
Canvas, 70 x 91 cm
London, National Gallery

Hogarth's reputation rests upon his
canvasses of moral subjects, or rather
the published engravings taken from
the paintings. The most famous series
were the Harlot's Progress, The
Rake's Progress, Mariage à la Mode
and the Election. They all demonstrate, in farcical detail, the merry duplicity inherent in avowedly moral
and Christian civilization. Hogarth
falls short of generalising his theme;
we are invited to laugh at a particular
individual whose weaknesses or mis-
fortunes lead him through the calami-
ties. The subject matter was taken up
by Cruikshank and Daumier in the
next century.

36. Sir Peter Lely
Two ladies of the Lake family, c. 1660
Canvas, 127 x 181 cm
London, Tate Gallery

Born in Germany, of Dutch parents,
Lely went to work in England where
he distinguished himself painting austere portraits at the court of Charles I.
In the more hedonistic court of
Charles II, Lely was appointed princi-
pal painter and turned his hand to
heroic admirals who had succeeded in
the wars against his own country of
Holland, and to the beautiful women
of the court preening and swooning
in affecting poses, as was the fashion.

35. Sir Joshua Reynolds
Age of Innocence, 1788
Canvas, 76 x 64 cm
London, Tate Gallery

One of the first to elevate painting to a respectable profession in England, Reynolds produced justifications for his ideas in the form of lectures on aesthetic theory. He mixes freely with the great writers and statemen of his time and enjoyed great acclaim for his portraits, which have paled over the years, and seem to us rather sentimental. His paintings are technically impressive but tend to leave an impression of emotional sterility. Can we doubt the sincerity of an artist who painted the wealthy classes as deserving and inoffensive beneficiaries of a nation's heritage?

37. Thomas Gainsborough
The morning walk, 1785
Canvas, 236 x 178 cm
London, National Gallery

Gainsborough was renowned for his stylish character-revealing portraits in which he chronicled the many faces of 18th century England – aristocrats, soldiers, statesmen, landowners, musicians and theatre folk. He painted over 700 in his lifetime. His best portraits are of women, and have a real French Rococo feel about them in their light, delicate grace and subtle nuances of colour and light. This elegant, upper class couple out for a stroll, are the newlyweds, Squire William Hallett and his bride, both aged 21. This painting demonstrates Gainsborough's technique of fluidly merging brushstrokes. The soft hair, glowing skin and fashionable dress of the couple is captured with the same skill as the dog and the hazy mass of trees behind.

38. Peter Paul Rubens
Rubens and Isabella Brant in the honeysuckle bower, 1609
Canvas, 178 x 136 cm
Munich, Alte Pinakothek

This painting commemorates Rubens' marriage to a woman about whom he wrote was, "without vices and was all goodness and sincerity". Of all the portraits done by Rubens this self-portrait is among the most arresting and psychologically profound. His wife has doubts, but he knows himself to be the master of his world. Rubens travelled extensively on diplomatic missions during which he painted the ceilings of palaces. He met the great names of his time, including Velasquez.

39. Peter Paul Rubens
The little fur, c. 1638
Panel, 176 x 83 cm
Vienna, Kunsthistorisches Museum

Rubens married his second wife, Hélène Fourment, when she was sixteen, and painted her here when she was a reputed twenty-four. It is thought that she tried to have this painting destroyed after his death. He stimulated a market for fleshy nudes and for rape scenes from mythology. While not denying that he was a great painter, it is easy to sympathise with the view that he was too often vulgar and insincere. We become voyeurs to a performance, not accidental observers to an intimate scene.

40. Sir Antony van Dyck
Portrait of Charles I, King of England, 1635-38
Canvas, 272 x 211 cm
Paris, Musée National du Louvre

Van Dyck was Rubens' chief assistant as a young man but he developed a celebrated career as a portrait painter. He travelled widely, particularly in Italy where he spent some time and found the greatest favour in the court of the English king. His portraits are sombre and guarded, seeming to idealize the sitter while retaining a little of the original character.

41. Frans Hals
Portrait of Catharina Hoeft and her nurse,
1619-20
Canvas, 86 x 65 cm
Berlin-West, Staatliche Museen,
Gemäldegalerie

Two travelling Dutchmen took the
Italian Baroque style to the Catholic
town of Utrecht in Holland. Here the
portraitist Frans Hals saw these new
styles. His group portraits of muske-
teers preparing to fight the Spanish
took on something of the Italian
chiaroscuro style in which shadowy
figures stand against a dark background.
Hals excelled at portraits of obvious
expression which makes him something of a sentimentalist. He ran a
large workshop and produced many
copies of the same work.

43. Jan Steen
Prince's Day, 14th November 1660,
c. 1668
Panel, 46 x 63 cm
Amsterdam, Rijksmuseum

Steen was an exceptional painter of
"genre" scenes, and ranks close to
Rembrandt. He did Biblical and
domestic groups and is best known
for his tavern scenes. He was a brewer
and innkeeper himself at times and
seemed to have delighted in the weaknesses of his fellow men for drink.
Steen proposed a merry world of jus-
tifiable corruption. Are we to believe
that the morality of the alehouse is in
accord with the religious beliefs of the
times? Scoundrels make entertaining
subjects for paintings.

42. Adriaen van Ostade
The violinist, 1673
Panel, 45 x 42 cm
The Hague, Mauritshuis

Ostade was a Dutch painter and print maker who excelled at small scenes of domestic life. His happy peasants disporting in an antique gloom are like stiff little wax dolls. His early figures tended toward caricature and were set in dark interiors, but he moved them out and introduced them to passing incidents like this visit from an itinerant fiddler. His brother Isack, became a distinguished painter of silver-white landscapes peopled with skaters.

44. Rembrandt Harmensz van Rijn
Danae, 1636
Canvas, 186 x 201 cm
Leningrad, The Hermitage

The Dutchman, Rembrandt, was a university educated man who absorbed the Caravaggio style of the Early Baroque. Some early paintings exploit the atmospheric use of shadowy light in scenes of scholars in cavernous cellars or studies. This painting has an overdesigned quality and looks back to Mannerism. A decade before, Rembrandt was taught by a belated Mannerist painter, Pieter Lastman. The movement of the girl, slowly turning in the bed to register gentle surprise at the entrance of the man, (recognisably Rembrandt himself) as he steals in behind the curtain, creates a powerful erotic moment, heightened by the effusive golden tones.

45. Rembrandt
The Night Watch, 1642
Canvas, 363 x 437 cm
Amsterdam, Rijksmuseum

There was a story that Rembrandt's decline and bankruptcy was on account of this painting, but there is no evidence that the company of soldiers who commissioned it ever rejected it, Even its popular name is an misleading addition. When the painting came to be cleaned it was found to be daylight. As with the famous painting, *The Anatomy Lesson,* it has a dry, noncommittal mood. It is an example of the move to photographic realism in painting, and perhaps Rembrandt's weaknesses were his reluctance to allow his own feelings to intrude into the painting. It remains a work of great technical mastery full of unusual light and sporadic action.

46. Jan Vermeer
The glass of wine, 1660-61
Canvas, 65 x 77 cm
Berlin-West, Staatliche Museen, Gemäldegalerie

Vermeer stands apart in his age as a great master whose innovations left scarcely a mark on the following generations. He painted a view of Delft, perhaps from a window, which had some influence on landscape painting, but his surviving works are nearly all of poised figures in quiet interiors. They hold wineglasses, jugs or musical instruments, and seem to converse in hushed words of intimacy.

47. Gerard Ter Borch
The letter, c. 1660
Canvas, 80 x 68 cm
London, The Royal Collection

Ter Borch's first drawing dates from his eighth year. In his teens he was visiting England, and was in Italy in his early twenties. For all his worldliness his paintings have a private, introspective atmosphere.
He had great skill in rendering fabrics; the lady's metallic dress seems so photographically real that it breaks the spell of the painting. The dog asleep on the little stool is a piece of charming invention, though the lady's feet are in a distorted perspective.

48. Franz Anton Maulpertsch
The Holy Family, 1752-53
Canvas, 127 x 90 cm
Vienna, Kunsthistorisches Museum

Maulpertsch was the leading Viennese painter of church frescoes. It is said that his style is a fusion of Rembrandt and the Venetian school. His inaccessible ceiling paintings are a complex arrangement of figures, lost in gloom and ghostly spaces, all cut with gleams and bursts of light. His subjects are the overpainted religious themes for which he showed little originality. One senses the routine repetition of religious decoration. Art becomes ritual. The true spirit of the Prussian Rococo is in this decorative determination.

49. Cosmas Damian Asam
Glorification of Mary, 1736
Fresco, detail
Ingolstadt, S. Maria de Victoria

The Asam brothers were a German
team of architects and frescoists who
learned their art in Rome. Bavaria,
where they worked upon decorating
church ceilings, followed the Italian
rather than the French Baroque. It is
said that German artists at this time
were using acid and unreal colouring,
while the Austrians took after the
Venetian palette, which is softer and
more romantic. It is difficult to under-
stand the high reputation of the Asam
brothers, from this detail of a famous
fresco. Their style was brittle and tended toward caricature.

50. Jean-Étienne Liotard
Portrait of a woman in Turkish costume,
c. 1749
Pastel on vellum, 100 x 75 cm
Amsterdam, Rijksmuseum

Liotard was a celebrated pastel artist
from Switzerland who became enamoured of everything Turkish after a
lengthy stay in Constantinople. His
paintings are smoothly appealing and
one, *La Belle Chocolatière,* of a lady
drinking chocolate was taken up by a
chocolate and cocoa company for
their printed cans. There are several
slightly different versions of this same
painting. It has an easy drawing-room
charm, and the affected pose of the
sitter is balanced by the pleasing effect
of the soft, white furnishings.

the Sistine Chapel. After the Italian experience his commissioned portraits and mythological decorations for palaces show the development of new techniques of brushwork.

The King of Spain sent him to Italy once more to buy paintings and to secure the services of Italian fresco painters for the King's palace. Velasquez befriended Poussin and Bernini, and collected paintings by Titian, Tintoretto and Veronese, the three great Venetian painters of the late Renaissance. It was while in Rome that he painted the celebrated portrait of the Pope Innocent X. It is said to be not a flattering painting: the Pope is depicted as thin-lipped and steely-eyed; his red cape is given a sheen of reflected light, which seems just that, until it is examined more closely, and then it is seen to be crude brushstrokes. It is characteristic of Velasquez' painting that the impressionistic effects are best observed from a distance.

Venus with a Mirror (The Rokeby Venus) might be of this time or even be earlier. The colour of the original has such a creamy, rich texture that it would seem to be nothing else than a membrane of skin over living flesh. Whereas the Giorgione *Venus* or Titian *Venus* each have a familiar reclining posture which may owe as much to the imagination of the painter as to the artist's model, this Velasquez *Venus*, with her startling posture, defies the imagination, and could only be from real life. It is a triumph of observation over convention. The only known Spanish nude painted until the 19th century, it takes a startling perspective on the human body, and robs the later Fragonard of what must surely be the most innocently provocative posture the human form can take.

With his last paintings, particularly *The Maids of Honour*, Velasquez showed himself a master of illusion, but an appreciation for this genius has come only in this last century, which has seen a rapid growth of interest in his work accompanied by an avaricious demand for his paintings at auctions. In this heady atmosphere of rediscovery, Velasquez has been called the greatest painter of all time.

The Maids of Honour, 1656
painting by Diego Velasquez
Madrid, Museo del Prado

CHAPTER V

Late Baroque and Rococo in Italy

Luca Giordano, the speedy Neapolitan – Maratta and Neo-classic nobility – Piazzetta and Tiepolo abandon Baroque for decorative Rococo style – Giovanni Tiepolo, master of illusionistic wall painting and the genius of Venetian late Baroque – Pietro Longhi and the funny absurd – The "vedute" or city views of Canaletto and Guardi – Piranesi and Pannini.

The Late Baroque saw a loosening of the styles begun by Caravaggio and the Carracci eighty years before. It was a slow evolution in the hands of many people, and it represents a step towards individuality. The structured tableaux of figures gave way to a looser scattering throughout the painting, which served to diffuse the central action. The unifying element in the picture was the decorative design. The figures began to luxuriate in a new freedom, to lean and stretch in a more languorous way, which hinted at the discredited Mannerist styles of a century earlier. Both the power of the Pope in Rome, and the strength of the Spanish hold on southern Italy diminished in the last decade of the High Baroque. France under King Louis XIV and the powers of the French Academy in Rome both became the significant influence in Italian painting. While some painters were still at work on derivative frescoes which look back to da Cortona, others were assembling the styles of the Rococo.

The first appearances of Late Baroque can be seen around 1660 in the frescoes of Mattia Preti (1613-99). He dominated the Naples school after Ribera with his dramatic, dynamic paintings. Luca Giordano (1632-1705), also from Naples, earned a reputation for his imitations of other painters; it is said that he could imitate Rembrandt's style. He was a nimble worker who could paint a huge altarpiece in one day. He went to Spain and left the Escorial Palace littered with his work. His manner was so varied that his work was called "confusionism".

In Rome Francesco Cozza painted the ceiling frescoes of the Pamphili Library with a free-ranging style. In the seaport of Genoa, Gregorio de' Ferrari and Domenico Pioli executed the finest Late Baroque ceilings. Giovanni Gaulli (1639-1709), called Baciccia, left Genoa for Rome and took the Baroque principle of illusionism to an extreme with the ceiling of the Gesù church in Parma. The fresco spills over the statues and painted plaster of the vault to complete the illusion of a crowd ascending into the blazing light of the sky.

Bernini was succeeded in Rome by Carlo Maratta (1625-1713). Maratta had no interest in the dramatic style of da Cortona and Baciccia; he had a classical leaning and developed a manner which has been called sweet and elegant, and which made him the most

The Archangel Michael drops the rebel angels into the fiery depths of hell, 1666
painting by Luca Giordano
Vienna, Kunsthistorisches Museum

Esther before Ahasverus, c. 1733
painting by Sebastiano Ricci
London, National Museum

Madonna del Carmelo, 1739, detail
painting by Tiepolo
Venice, Scuola del Carmine,
Sala Grande

celebrated ceiling frescoist of his times. The Neapolitan tradition was taken up by Francesco Solimena (1657-1747), who was described in his time as the greatest painter in the world, but whose work appears to us now as crowded and somewhat Mannerist. He was followed by Francesco de Mura (1696-1784) who grew away from the dark chiaroscuro to refreshingly bright colours, which earned him the name of the "Neapolitan Tiepolo". It was the northern Italian cities of Bologna and Venice which made the most successful attempts to break away from the classical Baroque. Giuseppe Maria Crespi, (1665-1747) refused to abandon the sharply contrasted chiaroscuro of Caravaggio, and painted domestic scenes which have a Dutch flavour. He became dissatisfied with Bologna and went to Venice where he influenced another emerging talent. Giovanni Battista Piazzetta, (1683-1754) studied under Crespi, and his paintings demonstrate a move away from Baroque contrasts and toward a more decorated Rococo style. The celebrated Venetian, Tiepolo, who completed the move to Rococo, is reputed to have been influenced by him.

Sebastiano Ricci (1659-1734) is said to have absorbed the style of the Neapolitan Luca Giordano, and yet his work is often scarcely distinguishable from that of the Venetian Veronese of a century earlier. He was commissioned in Rome, Florence, Parma and Vienna, and made journeys to England where he failed to be engaged to decorate St. Paul's Cathedral and Hampton Court Palace. His brilliant frescoes in the Palace of Medici-Riccardi in Florence are said to have given impetus to the Venetian school of decorative painting which spread all over Europe in the hands of Pellegrini, Pittoni and Tiepolo.

Giovanni Battista Tiepolo (1696-1770) was the culmination of this brief Venetian decorative era. He is said to be the master of the Italian Rococo style which can be seen as both a development from Baroque, and a reaction to it. Rococo had little hold on the imagination of Italian painters, it was principally a French and German phenomenon. It is characterized by the intrusion of decorative whimsy into paintings; by the use of silver and gold embellishments and sinewy countercurves. It was more a style for architecture and statuary than for painting.

Tiepolo moved away from the shadowy Caravaggist manner to a free and fluid style in which the figures are both decorative and amazingly real and alive. He sketched and painted at great speed, bringing the figures to life with highlights: touches of white, which give an illusion of movement. The work of Tiepolo and his Italian contemporaries is peopled with the costumed and masked figures of harlequins, and all the stock characters of an early theatre tradition called Commedia dell'Arte. Tiepolo's reputation suffered a decline through the 19th century, but his original, inventive designs, the vivacity of his work and the underlying sense of melancholy many people find in his paintings have rehabilitated his work in the eyes of the 20th century public. He is now often considered the greatest painter of his times. A possible pupil of Tiepolo, Pietro Longhi (1702-85), kept to Tiepolo's early style of genre painting, that is, figures grouped in a domestic

Interior of a prison, 1744-45
drawing by Giovanni B. Piranesi
Hamburg, Kunsthalle

scene. His works were popular and are to be seen in many galleries. His painting of a rhinoceros, a very artificial and wooden picture, is perhaps more famous than it deserves.

A more popular branch of Venetian painting are the townscapes; views of the city enlivened by outdoor activity; a regatta on a canal, a ceremony in a square. Outdoor views of Venice go back to Bellini and to Carpaccio who developed a brilliant technique of suffusing the atmosphere with indirect light. The city of Venice, set upon a Mediterranean lagoon, enjoys this characteristic powdery and yellow-tinted lighting we often see in the painting of Canaletto and Francesco Guardi.

Antonio Canal (1697-1768), called Canaletto, a prolific painter of Venetian city scenes would use a system of lenses called a camera oscura to throw an image of the city upon paper, which he then pencilled. These sketches formed the basis for a painting back at his studio. For a while he experimented with painting from real life, but the stern accuracy and photographic indifference of his subjects would suggest that he saw himself as a recorder of events rather than a creative interpreter.

Canaletto's commercial interests were advanced by the British Consul who decided upon the views to be painted and arranged for their sales. He may have also arranged Canaletto's visit to England, where he painted some rather beautiful views of London and the River Thames. His nephew Bernardo Bellotto (1720-80) took to painting views in Austria, Germany and Poland which are said to have great accuracy but are a little more sympathetic to figures; Canaletto tended toward wooden figures. Another painter of Venetian views, Francesco Guardi, (1712-93) married a sister of Tiepolo. He had not Canaletto's reputation, but a more recent appraisal of his work, particularly with regard to the impressionistic use of lighting, places him above Canaletto. The bright, pale colours and dashing character of his figures might owe something to Tiepolo. There is a sense of decorative fantasy about his paintings, which is firmly in the Rococo style.

A Roman style of townscapes focused not on the living city but on ruins. Piranesi (1720-78) was a Venetian architect who moved to Rome where he sketched and painted the disappearing Classical architecture. He is said to have prompted a visual interest in ancient cultures which illuminated the dull Latin literature that formed the basis of a European education. Pannini (c. 1692-1765/8) was another popular painter of ruins who was taken up by the French Academy in Rome and went to work in France. Whereas Pannini was precise and accurate, Piranesi introduced a poetic element that echoed through the later Romantic movement.

CHAPTER VI

Late Baroque and Rococo in France and England

Rigaud and Largillière - Pageantry and preening in the court of Louis XIV - The "fêtes galantes" of Watteau - Lancret and Nattier, his imitators - The pastels of Quentin de La Tour - Chardin; poetic realism amongst the pots and pans - François Boucher, the protegé of Madame de Pompadour - The virtuosity of Fragonard; his sketches and delicate colour harmonies - William Hogarth; satirical caricatures and moralizing "conversation pieces" - Sir Joshua Reynolds; Baroque portrait dignity and soft English landscape combined - The poetic mountain landscapes of Wilson, Cozens and Sandby - Thomas Gainsborough and fashionable portraiture - Joseph "Moonlight" Wright of Derby and the industrial landscape - George Stubbs, animal painter.

In the last years of the 17th century the French Baroque seemed stronger than ever. The Louis XIV style had brought an unprecedented sense of luxury, of gorgeous fabrics and posturing figures, in the commissioned paintings of Hyacinth Rigaud (1659-1743) and Nicolas de Largillière (1656-1746). Rigaud became a court flatterer and excelled in depicting shallow royalty as splendid majesty. One senses the constraints upon what must have been a sensitive artist, the obligation to paint dandies when his earlier work shows him to have been a skilled portraitist, owing something to Rembrandt. He is reputed to have painted over two thousand portraits but the majority of those were completed by the apprentices of his workshops. Largillière spent his formative years in Antwerp and in England as an assistant to Sir Peter Lely, the portraitist. When he returned to Paris to paint portraits of the wealthy middle-classes, his work retained the Flemish echoes. It required the determined genius of Watteau to soften the brittle French Baroque of the Louis XIV style.

Antoine Watteau (1684-1721) drew together the threads of French Baroque and produced a manner which was as distinctive and engaging as that of Tiepolo in Venice. It is a blend of Rubens and Veronese, often set against landscapes both rugged and lyrical. While the artists of France and Germany were elaborating the meaningless decorative impulse into something deeply and nostalgically human, his work retained the elements of the Rococo but seemed to provide an alternative: beautiful images of a delicate and ephemeral world.

Watteau trained with a designer and painter of theatrical scenery, at a time when the colourful Italian Commedia dell'Arte convention was being adapted for Parisian audiences. It can be no

King Louis XIV of France, 1701 painting by Hyacinthe Rigaud Chantilly, Musée Condé

Eight studies of a woman's head,
detail
drawing by Antoine Watteau
Paris, Musée National du Louvre

Resting shepherd
drawing by Nicolas Lancret
Vienna, Graphische Sammlung
Albertina

coincidence that many of Watteau's best paintings feature performers set against a backdrop which achieves a magical balance between painted scenery and awesome landscape. His celebrated cycle of three paintings on the same theme, *The Embarkation for Cythera*, features a band of happy little figures frozen in action while disporting under the protective spread of giant trees. Figures of women predominate, and men appear dressed as clowns or actors. There is something dreamlike about the scenes, something of sorcery, that puts us in mind of Shakespeare's later plays. The paintings were inspired by outdoor entertainments called *fêtes galantes*, in which the members of the French court would dress as peasants and take instruments out into the landscaped parks to act out antique fantasies of love and adventure. The paintings are set in the diffuse light of early morning or evening, and often with autumnal colours, suggesting departure, separation and melancholy.

Many of Watteau's paintings are linked by recurring figures which give a fortuitous sense of narrative and continuity. The painter had accumulated large sketchbooks of figures, and would draw from this store, often repeating his choice. He had a personal sense of colour; his silver-greys, mauves, and yellow-golds merge with olive-browns of the Dutch school, but because of his lack of interest in preparing a canvas with craftsmanship and mixing oils and pigments, his paintings are subject to deterioration. His reputation soared in his brief life and fell back with the changes in taste brought on by the Neoclassicists who dismissed his work as frivolous. Since that time we have learned to appreciate a strange wayward moodiness in his work, which was often the very essence of the 18th century.

Watteau had several imitators. Nicolas Lancret (1690-1743), who studied under the same theatre designer, Gillot, continued to paint *fêtes galantes* but failed to render the intangible moods and moved toward a delicate eroticism. Jean François de Troy (1679-1752) took the pastoral quality of Watteau and added the liveliness of Rubens' hunting paintings.

By this time, the ladies of the rustic paradise, bathing in ponds or asleep in bowers, had dropped most of their garments. Jean-Marc Nattier (1685-1766) made naked goddesses out of fulsome ladies. He was chief painter with special responsibilities toward the ladies of the Louis XV court. Nattier's son-in-law, Carle Van Loo (1705-65), also had a flair for flattering the ladies by presenting them as goddesses of mythology. His brother, Jean Baptiste Van Loo (1684-1745), spent time in London where his skill at catching unsparing likenesses in portraits displeased the English painters, except Hogarth, who took a particular interest in his methods. Many French painters continued unimpressed by Watteau's reverberating pageantry. Still-life and domestic scenes flourished under the brush of Jean Baptiste Chardin (1699-1779). His rather formal sense of naturalism served to counter the excesses of the Rococo style which predominated in his lifetime. Like Vermeer, he was intrigued by the possibilities of reflected light. His still-life paintings are particularly admired on account of a luminous depth

The girl with the marmot, c. 1785
watercolour by Jean Honoré
Fragonard
Vienna, Graphische Sammlung
Albertina

he imparted to fruit and bread and bottles of wine. It is now recognized that his portraits are superior to those of the over-praised Maurice Quentin de La Tour (1704-88). La Tour developed what became a Paris fashion for pastel portraits, but the public demand required something more glamorous than a clever likeness, so La Tour's technique became vulgar and obvious, to match the demand.

Two more convincing disciples of Watteau were two courtly decorators, François Boucher (1703-70) and Jean Honoré Fragonard (1732-1806). Boucher was a friend of Madame de Pompadour, the mistress of Louis XV, with whom he conspired to turn painting into an erotic confection. He obliged by producing pneumatic nudes with pink nipples tumbling upon unmade beds. It is a very commercial aspect of the erotic, with a little too much artifice and phony candour, and yet we are at a time when it is fashionable to deplore Boucher's blatant hedonism for its lack of redeeming social realism.

In his painting *Diana after her Bath* two improbable goddesses, who look as though they have never left Versailles, take a break from hunting to disrobe; no doubt a future age will look more kindly on the licentious conventions of Boucher's work. And it would be a pity if Boucher's other paintings were to be ignored; the crooked cottage among the trees of *Morning*, or *The Painter in his Studio*, which offers a surprising look of faraway regret upon the face of the painter seated at his easel.

Fragonard was briefly a pupil of both Chardin and Boucher, and like Boucher he became passionate over the work of Tiepolo. Fragonard was a rapid improviser whose work suffers through the unreflective bravura of his effort. He painted figures and landscapes, portraits and crumbling architecture, all with swift brushstrokes, and an impressionistic manner which brings his work perilously close to wallpaper decoration. It is the pure influence of Rubens untempered by the Dutch discipline. But his work matured as he came to admire Rembrandt and Hals, and in his thirties more sombre landscapes made their appearance alongside the lighter court pictures. He was commissioned to paint for Madame du Barry, the mistress of Louis XV, and it seems that his work fell out of favour with the growing Neo-classical fashion that took hold at the end of the 18th century. His last works show a move towards a Neoclassical style, but in the turbulent times of the French Revolution he adhered closely to his earlier techniques, and retired to the south of France to die.

In his earlier days Fragonard had travelled through Italy with a friend, Hubert Robert (1733-1808). Robert was a friend of Pannini and Piranesi, the painters of romantic ruins, and he excelled upon this subject, but softened the austerity of classical decay into images of a harmonious landscape. In this respect his work comes closer to that of Claude Lorraine. He returned to Paris and was appointed keeper of the King's pictures and an early curator of the Louvre. His range of subject matter widened to include the street scenes of Paris and large, decorative paintings for fashionable Parisian houses.

Portrait of David Garrick between
Tragedy and Comedy, 1760-61
painting by Joshua Reynolds
Private collection

The Baroque and Rococo styles which seem to be so
Mediterranean in character provoked a great deal of disgust and a
little envy across the channel in England. The 18th century had
opened upon a stilted tradition: portraits, some sporting scenes, a
few naval paintings, and very little of domestic vitality. There was
a passing fashion for decorative painting stimulated by the arrival
of French and Spanish artists, but it took a patriotic Englishman,
very distrustful of the French, to spark some life into English
painting.

William Hogarth (1697-1764), an irascible and pugnacious man,
began his career as a silver engraver. He moved on to become a
master at portraits and groups, and also a notable engraver of
satirical scenes for which he is best known. His influence on
English painting was seminal, for he became the centre of
opposition to the conservative tradition. He was scornful of a
fashionable appreciation for French painters and for old English
masters, critical of the high price these paintings fetched at sales.
His works break new ground and have a characteristic humour
and liveliness. They are said to show a debt to Rococo and to
Watteau. His sets of moral engravings, widely known today,
uncovering the follies of his times, are indicative of his highly
developed sense of social responsibility. They speak in negative
terms of the pitfalls awaiting a young man in a city – drinking,
gambling, corruption and prostitution. The wicked satirist's pen
may be a familiar feature today, but in the 18th century Hogarth,
along with his friends Henry Fielding, the author of Tom Jones,
and theatre actor David Garrick, were expressing a radical and
dissenting voice in a country of authoritarian duplicity in high
places. Hogarth's crusading fervour went a long way toward the
founding of the Royal Academy of Art in London and the

establishment of regular public exhibitions of paintings.

The English generation following Hogarth looked to Italy once more for inspiration. Allan Ramsay (1713-84) is credited with enlivening English portraiture with the more flamboyant Italian styles. The first president of the Royal Academy was Sir Joshua Reynolds (1723-92), who spent two years in Rome before travelling to the artistic centres of Northern Italy, Bologna, Florence and Venice. The Renaissance paintings of Titian, Tintoretto and Veronese made the profound impression on Reynolds which they had made upon earlier artists. His own portraits, once so dark and formal in the Van Dyck manner, took on the bright sweetness of the Italian Grand Style. He tried to reproduce the clear colours of the Venetian masters but his experiments resulted in a further paling of the paint so that we are left with ghost-like figures.

Reynold's style underwent further changes, perhaps for the worse, when in his late forties his work became excessively studied and classical. His historic pieces of this time are not his best. His portraits of children are tender and accessible, and their sweet sentiment has made them a popular decoration for chocolate boxes. Toward the end of his life a visit to Holland acquainted him with the Flemish master Rubens, and his own portraits took on some of the richer colours.

Reynolds was an educated and literate man who liked the company of intellectuals such as Dr. Johnson, the writer of a dictionary, and the statesman, Edmund Burke. He represented a new breed of cultured artists and was a believer in formal academic training. He was not a great draughtsman and his paintings are conventional and predictably charming. Only occasionally can we look past the surface of his portraits and into the character of the sitters.

From the mainstay of portrait painting two alternatives opened for English painters. An unexpected and lusty school of water-colourists flourished in the hands of Paul Sandby and Francis Towne. Sandby (1725-1809) painted landscape with a fidelity to asymetrical topography. He believed that the Welsh landscape was an excellent subject. Francis Towne had a more delicate and detached approach, and John Robert Cozens (1725-97), who chose the Alps as his subject, introduced poetic landscapes bathed in moody atmospheric light, which stirred similar passions in the next generation of oil painters.

Landscape painting became an acceptable subject. Richard Wilson (1713-82) was impressed by Italian painting in particular, and by the Frenchmen, Claude Lorraine and Poussin. His own moody landscapes with northern lighting are said to owe something to Albert Cuyp. He had a liking for rugged Welsh countryside and seemed to have made several paintings of similar views.

A more artificial approach to landscapes was developed by Thomas Gainsborough (1727-88). It would seem that he seldom took his canvas to the field but built up his picture from separate observations and from little models set up in his studio. It was not for another generation, and until the Romantics, that it was felt

Mary, Countess Howe, c. 1760
painting by Thomas Gainsborough
London, Kenwood House

Academy by candlelight, c. 1769
painting by Joseph Wright
London, Royal College of Surgeons
of England

legitimate for a wealthy man to involve himself in something remotely agricultural. Gainsborough's early landscapes painted in Suffolk, have affinities with 17th century Dutch painters. He later moved to a lighter style, closer to Watteau, and added groups of figures; his works show hints of Rococo design and a certain French atmosphere.

Gainsborough was obliged to give more time to portraits to make a living, and he took a liking to the works of Van Dyck, which, while making his work acceptable, cost his paintings something in originality. When Rubens became his model, his palette moved to richer, creamier hues. He was an original and inventive artist who devoted much time to the discovery of new techniques. Reynolds is supposed to have said of him: "Damn him, how various he is." His influence was considerable and his techniques were studied in depth by John Constable, who belongs to a later Romantic era of painting.

The long history of the Baroque casts a shadow which touches upon two of the last great painters of this genre. In a curious way they echo the two founders of Baroque, Caravaggio and the Carracci. Caravaggio's technique of chiaroscuro was taken up by Joseph Wright of Derby (1734-97). Wright had travelled in Italy and began his career painting moonlit landscapes and candle lit scenes which bring to mind the Utrecht school of Holland. He achieved many splendid and unforgettable paintings of curiously lit interiors, sometimes with the ruddy glow of firelight.

George Stubbs (1724-1806) was unimpressed by his travels in Italy. Like the Carracci, he believed that he should learn from observations of nature. He studied anatomy and lectured on medicine, and this led to his detailed paintings of horses, with a chilling over attention to muscles and the fine features of the anatomy. It is said that his preoccupation with horses stemmed from the time he saw a lion eating a horse in North Africa. There is something starkly classical in an artist who could pursue the ideals of realism to the dissection of his subjects, the horses. But then the whole era of the Baroque seems to have been a wavering contest between the two forces which contend for the creative soul of man, the Classical and the Romantic.

CHAPTER VII

Rococo decoration

Mirrors, furniture mouldings and porcelain – The great decorators of south German and Austrian churches – Maulpertsch and Asam – Liotard, romantic pastel painter – Goya's tapestries and his reaction to the Napoleonic invasion of Spain – His horror of anarchy and cruelty.

The Rococo style lent itself to the decoration of the new, lighter Parisian architecture, which superseded the Baroque excesses of Louis XIV's Palace at Versailles. Plaster moulding and fretwork were decorated in pastel colours, ivory-white, silver and gold, and interior decorators emphasised the spirit of light humour with the judicious use of mirrors. The spirit of Rococo is seen in the design of furniture and decoration of porcelain, in tapestries and silverware, and resoundingly, in the interior decoration of churches in southern Germany.

Franz Anton Maulpertsch (1724-96) was a leading Viennese frescoist who took his techniques to Czechoslovakia and Hungary. Cosmas Damian Asam, the Bavarian church decorator, painted frescoes of cluttered vulgarity, and Jean-Étienne Liotard (1702-89) was a Swiss painter in pastels, who became enamoured of Turkey and scandalized society by dressing in Turkish costume. He painted in Holland and England where his wicked likenesses displeased the sitters. His painting of the Countess of Coventry dressed up in Turkish costume occurs in very different reproductions, suggesting that copies were made by Liotard or others. The predominant whiteness shot through with blue of costume, carpet and furniture fabric, all suggest a very modern sensitivity to fashionable decoration.

The Rococo current continued in France through the period of the French Revolution and overlapped with Neoclassicism in painting and decoration. Spain was a little touched by the Rococo, but the overwhelming factors of war and invasion prevailed upon painting styles. In the tradition of individualists and eccentric geniuses like El Greco and Velasquez, a new name arose in Spanish painting, that of Francisco Josè de Goya y Lucientes (1746-1828), known as Goya. He spent time in Rome but came back to Spain to begin his career at a time when Tiepolo, who had lived for a year in Madrid, was the most celebrated painter. Goya's designs for tapestries have something of Tiepolo's affected gaiety, and were soon modified under the direction of the German artist, Anton Raphael Mengs (1728-79), to reflect a renewed international interest in classical art. It was not long before he broke with Meng's academic form of classicism. Goya was a powerful personality who found himself drawn to the work of Rembrandt and Velasquez. His own individuality began to assert itself, along

Ornament of the Hall of Mirrors in the Amalienburg, 1734-39 after a drawing by François Cuvillies Munich, Nymphenburg Park

The Duchess of Alba, 1795
painting by Francisco de Goya
Madrid, Duke of Alba collection

with a sense of realism and a pride in direct observations. For all this his earlier portraits are stern and stiff. He caught the unsavoury character of the sitters but felt unwilling to give them a dynamic, living form. His portrait of the Duchess of Alba (1795) is of a doll-like figure with an expression of distrustful superiority. Under successive kings Goya became a successful and fashionable court painter, and might have remained so had he not been tormented by two events. At the age of forty-six he fell ill, and it left him totally deaf. His sharp and discerning eye came under the influence of a feverish imagination. His work aspired to the kind of subjects for which there are never commissions. He painted a madhouse, and made a series of engravings attacking the abuses of organized religion and politics. Pressure from the Inquisition and the authorities caused him to withdraw the plates of the engravings, and hand them over to the king. Even his religious paintings reflected a starkly new attitude, one of artistic integrity, and his portraits turned to a form of realism which borders on caricature.

The second event which profoundly redirected Goya's life was the French invasion of Spain under Napoleon. The English under Wellington finally liberated Spain and Goya made a fine portrait of the Duke. But widespread cruelties and the general suffering of war had affected Goya and prompted him to produce a series of horrific etchings under the title *The Disasters of War*, besides the harrowing paintings of the executions, and further portraits, less-than-flattering likenesses of the tyrant who now ruled Spain. His final works speak of his misery and despair. He returned to Bordeaux in France, where he died.

Goya's work comes close to the modern interpretation of an artist's work as an illumination of life. He was faithful to his times and earned respectability for the role of the artist as a reformer. He had no obvious successors in Spain, but his work influenced Delacroix and the 19th century French movement, as well as the later schools of Romanticism, Realism and Impressionism.

Bibliography

The author has consulted the following works in the writing of this book:

Painting and Sculpture in Europe, 1780 to 1880 *by F. Novotny*

Baroque and Rococo *by Germain Bazin*
Baroque and Rococo Art *by Erich Hubala*
The Baroque Painters of Italy *by Charles McCorquodale*
Rococo to Revolution *by Michael Levey*

Watteau *by Helène Adhémar*
David to Delacroix *by W. Friedlander*
Larousse Encyclopaedia of Renaissance and Baroque Art.
Art and Architecture in Italy 1600-1750 *by Rudolf Wittkower*